Driftwood

A Collection of Works

By

Violet Overmyer

Presented by

Brass Hinge Publishing

Driftwood

A Collection of Works

By
Violet Overmyer

© 2010 Brass Hinge Publishing

ISBN-13: 978-0983159001
(Brass Hinge Publishing)

ISBN-10: 0983159009

Note:

The poem "Trees" by Joyce Kilmer is in the public domain and may be reproduced without permission.

Dedication

This book is dedicated to the family and friends of Violet Overmyer. We only wish that she were here to be a part of her life long dream of having her work published. May her words touch your heart.

Table of Contents

Quacker House The Raising of Six Ducks

Table of Contents Continued

Poems

Preface

I remember walking the shoreline of many rivers, lakes, and reservoirs. Every excursion was an adventure for the kid in me. The warm sun would find me Skipping rocks, fishing, or just plain old-fashioned lazy day loafing. I can remember one thing that seemed to be so prevalent. On the untouched banks, there would be pieces of curled and odd shaped chunks of wood. They resembled pieces of limbs or possibly roots from a tree long since fallen. Each piece of wood had it's own character... a story to tell... a unique mystery about the way it looked. I would rescue them from the ebbing water and brush them off. The more I brushed the more I could see what a prize I had just found. These marvels of time and Mother Nature are known as driftwood. Each was holding a certain beauty unlike any other I had found. If I had just kept them all, I would have a room full of marvelous and eccentric charm. It would be a collection of wonderment and awe for many to share. Nevertheless, "Woe is me", for I let them slip away. They returned to their journey. Drifting aimlessly into the lives of others. Enlightening imaginations in the same way they had done mine. Lost but not forgotten. Now, only memories... refined remembrances...yes just as the name implies...Driftwood.

I was given a copy of works penned by Violet Overmyer during the late 1930s through the late 1950s. In the not so technological past, this manuscript was fashioned into a self made book.

Violet had always wished to have her work published and printed in true book form.

After reading her work, I realized I had been given another chance to do something special with what seemed so much like the Driftwood from years ago. I could unlock a nearly forgotten, unique, and charming piece of yesteryear. Yes indeed, a prize unto itself.

I never met Violet Overmyer. She passed on in the years before I came to know her work. Having read her work, I now have a better understanding of who this woman was and what she represented. She is special too…the same as those rare pieces of driftwood…bits of art, which perked my imagination so many times.

I have assembled Violet's works into this book. The title "Driftwood" just seemed appropriate. It is rare and unique, yet not to be forgotten. Her passion for life and her love of writing shine through in this collection. Enjoy her award winning poetry and her lovable story, "Quacker House The Raising of Six Ducks".

Stephen J. Flitcraft (Owner)

Brass Hinge Publishing

BATH DAY AT QUACKER HOUSE

Have you ever seen six ten-day old, yellow ducklings take a bath for the first time in a four-inch deep pan of water? It is a riot!

They had been unusually daring and pestiferous all morning. The bugs in the backyard were too hard to locate or lacked that savory flavor which the ones beyond the fence had. **In** any case, I had "switched" them back to their own locale three times and on three other searches had found them around in front of the house. Something had to be done.

I filled a fifteen-inch square pan with two buckets of water and called for them to come. They, at the time, were curled up under the lounge and ignored all my pleas. I went on with my work.

Minutes later, I checked again to find them scouring for bugs in Mr. Rust's backyard. I herded them back to the pan. They looked at it warily. It was new and it might be dangerous. Finally, one craning neck detected the glimmer of water and came closer. This action prompted two others to edge nearer, one of whom was querulously calling, "What is it? What is it?"

The daring one dunked his bill. "Hey, fellas, it's water. A whole bathtub of water! "

They all crowded around the pan with breasts pushed over the rim and bills dipping into the liquid.

"Didya ever see so much water? We'll never be able to drink all this."

Naturally, with so much crowding, somebody would have to fall in. It was a new experience. Two little webbed feet began flailing the water and the wobbly yellow body became a flying dart. Its speed carried the body right over the edge into the shrieking crowd.

"Help! Help! Something is in there. It'll get us!" And off they took with craning necks and eyes fearful. All but one and that was the one who had fallen in. He thought it was worth a repeat performance and back he came. When he started back, the others stopped their flight and watched, then edged closer again. Soon a second one was over the rim and into the water. A similar fit of passion hit this one and he, too, darted across the pan and right over the edge, sending the uninitiated into a squawking retreat.

"Hey, fellas, that was fun!" and back he came. This time four dared the dangers of the unknown. Such a splutter and splashing and flipping of water you haven't seen in a long time.

It would have been a regular "Saturday-bath", had not one of them yelled, "Watch out! I'm a speedboat!" and over the rim they went calling for protection. At last, all six got in and had a thorough cleansing. They flipped their heads in joy.

Finally, the bath was over and they all came over to my chair and "toweled" themselves dry. The duck fuzz on their back shed the water well, but their tummies were sopping wet. How do you get the moisture out of a feather pillow? Well, these tads used their heads. Each worked on his own tummy, running his bill through the fuzz and squeezing out the water.

Now the novelty has worn off. They are still making their forays into the neighbor's yard to hunt for bugs. Then, they become tired and curl up under my chair and sleep. On their way, they frequently stop by and take a sip of their bath water, but one might say that bath day at Quacker House is over.

SIX QUACKS

It was near the end of May, which is spring of the year here in Northern Indiana. Our days of arduous work of grading final exams, averaging grades, issuing report cards and generally completing all which the administration required was over. My friend, a co-worker, and I were seeking rest and relaxation by driving some forty miles to the "big city". We'd have a day of shopping and looking. (Mostly Looking) We had no real reason for going except to "kick up our heels" so to speak. The daily grind of "8 to 4" was over for a few months. We were exhilarated by the freedom, so much so that my brain may have been addled.

On our journey, we noticed on the left hand side of the highway, a freshly painted sign, printed in bold letters "B-a-b-y D-u-c-k-s for sale".

"Oh, let's stop to see them on our way back!" I have since learned, these impulsive sightings often do me in. It was surely true this day.

Soon we returned from the city. "We stopped to see the baby ducks. May we?"

"Come this way," said an old man whose figure was dressed in faded blue shirt and overalls. "Right here in the barn."

"Ah-h-h, baby ducks! Aren't they darling?" My eye had caught sight of them, maybe fifty, maybe a hundred in the dimly lighted barn.

"Just one day old", said the owner as he picked one up and placed it in the palm of my hand. A smart salesman, that one! He let the duck sell itself. As soon as that tiny, warm ball of yellow fuzz relaxed in my hand and those two black beads for eyes looked me over, the sale was clinched.

"How much are they?" I do not remember the figure he quoted but I do recall saying, "I'll take six, this one and five others".

Six ducks. Six day-old baby ducks! What does a school teacher with one house and one garage, no sheds, no barns, no pens and just recently released from the long winter's grind of teaching school to seek rest and relaxation mean by saying, "I'll take six!" What does she MEAN?

By now, you know my brain was addled. It was the beginning of an interesting experience.

QUACKER KITCHEN

On the way home with the small box containing six little noisy things cradled on my lap, this conversation took place:

"Where are you going to put them?" It was a bit of a jolt to realize that I was so ill prepared. Finally, after putting my hand in the open-topped box to calm the ducks, "I'll get a cardboard box out of the basement."
"Where are you going to put the box? They must be kept warm. These May nights are cool."
Suddenly as though a light dawned, "I'll just have to keep them in the kitchen."
Explosively, "In the kitchen?" Then kindly after a few moments of silence, "What will you feed them?" "We'll have to buy some milk." As time went by, bread, oatmeal, And a long list of other things were added.

As soon as the car rolled to a stop in my own driveway, those six little, animated fuzzies were up and chatting. It didn't take long to place a half-inch thick layer of newspapers on the floor with the big box from the basement on top of them. We had some difficulty maneuvering around the box because it didn't seem to fit anywhere in that small kitchen. However, they had to be kept warm, didn't they?

We ran a heavy extension cord from the one wall plug in the room across the floor to a sturdy lamp, which we put in the box. This should keep them warm at night. Of course, we had to remember to step across the extension cord every time we went from the kitchen to any other part of the house. If we didn't, it would upset either the lamp or us. A small can lid served to hold the drinking water except that the ducks kept stepping on the edge of the can lid and upsetting what was in it. It required constant refilling.

After warming the milk, we dipped small pieces of bread in it and put them in a second can lid. They were ravenous but soon their hungry squawks lessened and then stopped.

Everything worked well, Considering.

We were to learn a lot in the next three months. In fact, it had already started.

Lesson number 1... Don't be so impulsive!

QUACKS FIRST DAY

Early the next morning, long before the first rays of light streaked the eastern sky, my mind was jerked into alertness by the thought of ducks. I listened. No sound. Were they all dead? Had they gotten too much heat from the lighted lamp in the box? Had they gotten too little heat and all chilled to death?

"Slip out quietly and check on them and then come back to bed," I told myself without uttering a sound. It didn't work out that way. In the two seconds it took me to get to the kitchen, one little fellow was already up and started "yak, yak, yakking" as soon as he saw me. He seemed to say, "Hi, I'm hungry! When do we eat?"

Soon five others were up stretching first one leg far out behind and then the other. They, too, joined in the chorus. "I'm thirsty!" "I'm hungry!" "Get things going"?

The process of the night before was repeated. Warm the milk, break up the bread, dip the pieces in the milk, and put it in a clean can lid. The other was soiled with excrement, as was the floor of the box. There's more to raising ducks than just glibly saying, "I'll take six!"

This sunless day dawned cloudy and cold. The spring-like weather of the previous day seemed to recede into the chill of winter. There would be no outdoor activity for these little babies today. However, they weren't too restless.

After their meal, they squatted around

the drinking cup and took sips quite frequently, sometimes just running the water through their bills and letting it spill on the floor. There just was not room for all six to cluster around the drinking cup, which meant that one or two were forced to remain outside the circle and they, too, wanted water now and then. Those little webbed feet didn't care what they walked in or on. Often one of the outsiders would step on one of the resting ducks that, in turn, got up with a squawk. Now there were four webbed feet moving across the cup. Usually one of those feet would catch the rim of the cup and the whole thing would be turned over. When one of the ducklings squatted right down in the water, I knew it was time to do something. The problem was soon remedied with a quart jar full of water turned upside down in a small pan. It served well during those early days.

Cleanliness was another problem. Certain it is, that if anything drank as much water as they did, it had to come out somewhere. Affectionately I called them my six little squirts. Ducks and geese are well known for this, with the latter being worse than the former. Still, those six must have been close to the record-setters of the duck family. Constant cleaning couldn't keep up with them. By the end of the first day, my kitchen had lost its appetizing aroma.

QUACKER CRUMBS

Each passing day brought changes. The ducklings no longer waited for me to start a leisurely day. They began giving orders. "Get up! We're hungry!" And, they were hungry, always hungry. The milk and bread routine soon changed to cooked oatmeal and milk with a few straggled ends of bread thrown in. This, too, was subject to change since the oatmeal box was getting close to the empty mark.

At a co-op house in a not-too-distant city, I purchased a large sack of "mash", a special preparation for growing ducklings. They liked it very much and ate more and more, cramming it in by bobbing their heads up and down until their throats were distended.

In between regular feedings during those early days, they hunted for bugs and things in the grass of the backyard. It was a joy to watch them spot some flying insect and with head and neck stretched far forward and close to the ground, chase after it. After each feeding or bug-catching expedition, they returned to the drinking fountain to wash things down. With all this eating and drinking, they grew.

The first week they were out of the kitchen during the daylight hours only, but from then on, they were outside night and day. A wire pen kept them confined during the day. A little house, in which they were locked at night, protected them from marauders, man, or beast.

As time went by, other supplements were added to their diet. A good friend regularly brought the ducks discarded lettuce and cabbage leaves, carrot tops, and other unsalable vegetables.

With bugs and ants and worms and discarded vegetables, one would think that ducks would eat anything. These ducks wouldn't. By the time, the first big sack of mash, purchased in a town some fifteen miles away, was almost empty; I decided to get the second sack at a nearby feed store.

One morning I opened the sack, filled the trough with the new food, and returned to the house to work. Soon the squawking started and then became much louder. One duck can make a lot of noise if she has a mind to do so, but six soon turn it into a din! Some neighbor would be reporting me to the local police.
The trough was still full, barely touched. The ducks, huddled in one small space with heads and necks high, continued to shout, telling me, in no uncertain terms, that they did not like the food, they would not eat it, and they were hungry!
What could be done? I drove the fifteen miles to the town where I had made the original purchase and the fifteen miles back to get a sack of food they liked. It stopped the squawking as soon as they tasted it.
I was their friend again.

THE QUACKER'S

SITTERS

In those days, teachers in our area were expected to teach all winter long. Spend their summers either attending college. Improving themselves by taking educational trips somewhere so that they would be more interesting in the classroom the following winter. Previous summers had found us in New York, Montreal, the Midwest, Colorado, the southwest and California.

This duck-raising summer was no exception. We were expected to go to earn educational points! What do you do with six growing ducks while you are away? In such cases, it is nice to have a kind and generous sister and brother-in-law on whom one can impose. They lived in the same small town.

After much careful planning prior to the day of our departure, we moved the pens, food, duck shelter, and, of course, the six ducks from my lot to my sister's house.

Leaving all our duck-raising cares and woes in capable hands, we soon departed for the far northwest. The three-weeks trip took us through the Midwest to Yellowstone National Park and then on to Glacier National Park with a return trip through southern Canada. How educational it was or how useful in the classroom is debatable but it was enjoyable. I well remember writing my sister about the bears, especially the cub bears that we saw in Yellowstone Park. I told her that next summer I planned to raise six bear cubs instead of six ducks and was she interested in being a sitter for them. She didn't reply to such asininity.

Along the way, we had continued reports of the ducks' well being, but I didn't learn until we were back home again that my sister had had a most unusual problem.

Early one morning she went outside to check on the ducks and to feed them. With much yak-yak-yakking, they let her know that they were glad to see her and to be fed and watered. She counted them and there were six. In the following quotes, she will tell her own story:

"Later I passed the pen and quickly counted. Lo and behold! One was missing. I counted again. There were only five ducks. I was dumbfounded. Vi would be home from her trip soon. What would I do? I called my husband and said, "Frank, one duck is missing!" We both walked hurriedly to the lake, thinking the missing duck could have slipped under the fence and wandered toward the water. No duck! I walked around the yard and up the street. Surely if some animal had gotten it, there would be feathers. Nothing! No evidence of any kind was visible. It had vanished in thin air. Wondering what I should do, and deeply puzzled, I returned to talk again with my husband. Maybe he had discovered something. Still nothing! It is putting it mildly to say, that we were upset. Walking back to the duck pen, I counted again. One, two, three, four, five, SIX! They were all there! A small boy stood near the pen.

"My mother wouldn't let me keep him".

"Mom, They've got so many ducks; they won't miss one"!

"Honey, take him back. Even if they had a thousand, he is not yours. You must not take things that don't belong to you.

'But Mom!" "

"Mrs. Mclane, would you give me one?"

"They aren't mine to give. I am just taking care of them until my sister gets back."
"

" I was surely glad to see that duck. The other ducks were glad too and greeted him with, "Quack, quack, quack; we're glad you're back".

"Back Home Again In Indiana." We always sing this when our car crosses the state line as we return from out-of-state travels. The trips are wonderful but it is even better to get back home again.

We arrived in our own little community about nine-thirty at night. We drove immediately to my sister's house. All was dark. They had retired for the night. I just had to see the ducks; so, with a flashlight in hand, we walked to the backyard. Turning the spotlight on them, I was shocked!

"These aren't MY ducks! Where are MY ducks? What's happened?" These ducks were great big ducks, pure white and fully feathered out. Their wing feathers were long and strong. My ducks were yellow and fuzzy.

"They have to be my ducks. Alice wouldn't be taking care of ducks belonging to anyone else." And, of course, they were. I remembered them as I had last seen them. They certainly had grown in those three weeks of our travels.

Back in their own backyard, they

continued to eat and to grow, not so much in size as in developing the characteristics of adult ducks and drakes. Four of them were ducks with loud, raucous voices, which disturbed the nearby neighbors, who told me about it. The two drakes had raspy, squeaky voices and had developed curls in their tail feathers. All of them went through a molting period, which left a mass of feathers all over their pen.

The summer would soon be gone. What would become of my ducks? I wouldn't consider eating them. They were my friends! They had brought me so much joy. Could I give them to someone who would promise not to eat them? I wanted them to have a full adult life and not come to some untimely end. At least, I did not want to know about it if they did.

On one trip around the lake, we saw a farm with a small stream running through the property. The ducks would love this. The people living on the farm were acquaintances and were very nice. They had small children who would enjoy the ducks. I called the lady and explained how she might have six free ducks. Her response was negative. "We are moving into town next month."

Time was growing short. We were down to our final ten days before school would start and the problem was still unsolved.

A visiting friend, hearing our tale of woe, asked, "Why don't you try Story Land Zoo in South Bend?" Story Land Zoo. Twice we had picnicked there, paid the small fee, and strolled through the enclosed area where many types of animals and birds had their own pens. The ducks even had their own swimming pool.

"Do you suppose they would take them?" This solution sounded too good to be true.

The friend replied, "It wouldn't hurt to try". We made a hurried forty-mile trip to talk with the manager. "Would you like to have six healthy, white ducks to add to your collection?"

"Why, yes. We'd be glad to take them."

STORY LAND ZOO

Story Land Zoo, dedicated in 1957 to the children of the Valley of Promise, is a fabulous place for the young in years and the young at heart.

One small part of a vast acreage of wooded land comprises Story Land Zoo. There are two main buildings, a cleverly designed entrance house, representing a dwelling, and a much larger shiny red barn with white trimming around the doors and windows.

Inside the six-foot high fence in their own individual pens and cages are the animals and birds of the zoo.

Walkways take interested persons from one pen to another.

Here are the Emveo children and their grandmother just entering the gate. Let's fall in behind them and listen.

"Are we going to see lions and tigers?" asks Jeffie, who is a sturdy six years old?

"I want to see a "tagger"," says Susie, just three.

"Susie, say tiger."

"That's what I said, Gramma. Tagger!"

" Hello, good-looking'! Awrk! Awrk! Hello, good-looking'!"

"That's the parrot, Allie. He must be talking to you. See his pretty colors."

" Hello, Good-looking'! Awrk!"

"Gramma, what does that sign say?"

" Candy Cane Ranch, dear, and that big animal with its long neck is a llama."

" Look at his long nose and mouth. They're pointed and watch how he chews his hay. Isn't that funny?"

" I can chew that way," says Jeffie. "Just watch me".

"Don't do it, Jeffie. You may hurt your jaw."

" But I can."

" You can't," says Susie ", your mouth goes up and down. His goes from side to side."
"

" Stop arguing children. Look over there at the baby llama."

" This one's ears are back."

" That's the mama llama and she is disturbed. Let's go to the next pen."

" Oh, I know what that is. Look, Susie, that's a lamb and isn't its coat a shiny black?"

" See that rhyme printed on the board. Does anyone know what it says?"

" Yes, Gramma," Jeffie replied, "I can read. That says, Baa, baa, black sheep. Have you any wool? Yes, sir, yes, sir. Three bags full."

" Isn't that a nice little house for the lamb?"

" Come on, children; let's go to the barn next, to see the cow and calf."
"   " Oh, look at the pictures on that sign! I can't read it. There aren't any letters on it."
" That's a cat playing a violin, and that's a full moon with a cow over it, and that's a dog."
" What is it Gramma?"
"That is another nursery rhyme. It starts out 'Hey, diddle, diddle. The cat and the fiddle. The cow jumped over the moon. The little dog laughed to see such sport."

" Oh, that's a dish pulling a spoon along. That's nice. Mommy will have to come to the zoo."

" That cow has a wet nose. Gramma, will it bite? It's smelling, Susie."

" No, dear, cows don't bite."

" That's the closest I've ever been to a cow."

" Come, children. There's one more nursery rhyme Jeffie must read."

" That little building has a bell on top. Why, Gramma? Do they ring the bell?"

" That represents a school building".

"My school doesn't look like that." Said Jeffie.

"Well, long ago, the school building had

just one room."

"Oh, there's a lamb, a white lamb!"
Read what it says Jeffie."

" Ba-a-a."

"Gramma, that was the lamb calling.
It's lonely."

" Mary had a little lamb. Its fleece
was white as snow."

" Oh, I know the rest of it. Gramma,
can't we show Daddy and Mommy the
zoo?"

I believe that the Emveo children
and their grandmother enjoyed it.

We are going to leave them now to
report hurriedly that there is a bear in
a cage, monkeys in another, many
deer, goats, pigs, and donkeys besides
many different kinds of birds. But, as
Susie calls it, there is no "tagger".

My main interest, of course, was the
duck pen. Some eighteen to twenty
occupants of various breeds and
sizes had their own fifteen-foot
swimming pool with a diving board
extending over the water. Here, they
might rest or dry off. Small bushes at
the water's edge protected them from
too much sun.

This would be the home for my
ducks.

THE LAST QUACK

Shortly thereafter, (very shortly) my friends, the ducks, and I would be parting company. Misgivings? Yes, a few but there were no other way. It had to be. What better solution could there be than Story Land Zoo? Where a constant stream of visitors in the summertime would enjoy the antics of my ducks?

The final four days came. School would start on Thursday with a shortened day. The principal's meeting would open at nine and books would be issued to the students that afternoon. By three o'clock, we would be free to transport the ducks to their new home.

All day Monday, Tuesday, and Wednesday the ducks and I enjoyed each other's company. After breakfast each day, they were free to do as they wished. No restrictions, except to stay out of the neighbor's yard and to keep out of the street in front of the house. They roamed the yard hunting for bugs and ants. They waddled up and down each bean row of my garden, gobbling up what I hoped was bugs but were probably succulent green beans. They swam in their pool and went through their usual ritual of drying and preening.

With an armload of books and writing materials, I stretched out in a lounge chair under a shade tree and kept watch. Frequently they returned to the drinking fountain, which was near my chair, to get a sip of water. When one started for a drink, they all came, chatting among themselves. Finally, tired of hunting and full of bugs or beans, they squatted under and around my chair. They tucked their bills under their wings and took a long nap. One, directly in my sight, probably the one on guard duty, without making any other movement, opened one eye, looked the situation over, saw that all was quiet, and closed it again.

Thursday was a different day since I was at school. My neighbors reported that for hours the ducks walked the fence line of their pen calling, constantly calling.

How could we transport them to their new home? They certainly wouldn't fit in that small box which I had cradled on my lap a few months ago.

We borrowed a crate from a local hatchery, put the ducks inside, put the crate in the trunk of the car with the lid up, and went squawking toward our final destination.

People along the way, surprised at the noise, looked up smiling and waved.

Arriving at Story Land Zoo, we asked for the manager. "We're here with the ducks."

"Great! I'll be right with you."

He placed the crate on a little trailer behind a small tractor and asked us to follow him. After lifting the crate over the fence into the duck pen, he opened the lid. Immediately three heads on three long necks popped out to look things over. Gently he lifted them out one by one and set them on the ground. We watched. How would they react to their new home?

The duck pen had been a relatively quiet place as we approached. Some were quietly swimming in the water. Two were asleep on the edge of the pool. Others, which had recently been swimming stood on dry land preening and oiling their feathers. Suddenly pandemonium broke loose. My ducks had never seen so much water.

"Hey, fellas, look at that ocean!"

Squawking and spreading their wings, they literally flew into the water and across the pool. They acted like delinquent teenagers! The frightened residents, which joined in the squawking, scrambled out of the pool, and cowered along the fence line. My ducks, still shouting raucously, raced back. One big black and white duck, which by its mannerisms said, "I'm not going to let a

bunch of bullies take over," slid into
the pool. As one of mine raced by, he
gave a mighty peck, which took out a
bunch of white feathers.

"Ouch! That hurt!"
    The big duck then took after another
one. After about ten minutes of wild
activity, the pecking order had been
established and peace was restored.
    Quieting down, my ducks were still
joyously swimming in the water, even
turning their bottoms up to search for
things below the surface.
    The time for parting had come. Misty
eyed, I said to myself, "goodbye,
friends," and turned away.

Poems

I have selected Joyce Kilmer's famous poem
"Trees" as an introduction to my own poetic efforts.
Note the underscored line. Perhaps this applies to me.

TREES

I think that I shall never see
A poem lovely as a tree.

A tree whose hungry mouth is prest
Against the earth's sweet flowing breast;
A tree that looks at god all day,
And lifts her leafy arms to pray.

A tree that may in summer wear,
A nest of robins in her hair.
Upon whose bosom snow has lain.
Who intimately lives with rain.
<u>Poems are made by fools like me,</u>
But only God can make a tree.

I have selected Joyce Kilmer's famous poem
These magnificent thoughts were memory passed when a
Note the reference used here evident English appeal to the

TREES

I think that I shall never see
A poem lovely as a tree.

A tree whose hungry mouth is prest
Against the earth's sweet flowing breast;
A tree that looks at God all day,
And lifts her leafy arms to pray;

A tree that may in Summer wear
A nest of robins in her hair;
Upon whose bosom snow has lain;
Who intimately lives with rain.
Poems are made by fools like me,
But only God can make a tree.

A POWER DIVINE

*This trilogy on "Spring", "Summer", and "Winter", tied
for first prize In the long lyric group and was published
in the 1942 "Patrons-of-Poetry Anthology of Northern
Indiana Poets competition sponsored by the Progress
Club of South Bend, Indiana.*

SPRING

The harsh cold winds of winter's blast;
Swept forth o'er prairies wide.
Congealing in its icy clutch
The barren countryside.
The leafless trees with broken limbs
Creaked sadly as they swayed.
The little brook with frozen lip
No voice of welcome made;
Above the earth a murky sky
Cast flakes of ice and snow;
And hope within the human heart
Was ebbing with its flow;
When suddenly a still small voice
awoke each sleeping thing
And through a hushed, expectant night
God spoke and it was spring.
And thus, dear Lord, for bursting flowers;
For budding, shady trees;
For fresh, green grass; refreshing showers;
A warm and gentle breeze;
A clear bright sun in heaven's blue,
And brooks that wind the lea;
But most of all for hope renewed,

We offer thanks to Thee.

SUMMER

With springtime's, call each bulb and seed,
pushed forth a tiny root.
With firm lips pressed to nature's breast
to feed a growing shoot.
Beneath the summer's glowing sun,
the fruit trees blushed with bloom.
As honey bees with gold-stocked legs
waxed drunk on bud perfume.
The hot dry winds of mid-July,
Caressed the fields of grain.
And turned a waving, green-capped sea
into a golden plain.
This miracle from death to life,
a rich and verdant one.
Is far beyond the powers of man.
God smiles and it is done.
Oh, Father God, the summertime
brings countless things to praise.
The wondrous sights that fill the night;
the beauties of our days.
A woodland flower; the bobwhite's call;
The lonely bumblebee.
A thousand words could not express
our humble thanks to Thee.

WINTER

And now, at last, the time of rest
Descends o'er dell and steep.
Wise Mother Nature takes her brood
And cuddles them to sleep;
She cools the day and lengthens night;
A southern sun swings low
As she implants each baby seed
Beneath her cloak of snow.
O'er all the earth falls quietness
As tiring labors, cease
And nature rightly claims her due
A wealth of rest and peace.
A lasting peace, an aim of man,
Has never yet been won,
But that we might approach this goal,
God gave the world His Son.
O, Lord, the Christ-child gave us faith
To brave the needs of life.
He brought us hope by giving strength
Through human ills and strife.
He promised us a future land
When death has made its claim.
O, Father God, for this great gift
We praise Thy holy name.

POISON IVY

Here lies my pose
Beneath a curse
Because I found
Your presence rich;
And since I go
From bad to verse,
I must admit
For I ITCH!

- Published in the 1937 "Patrons-of- Poetry Anthology of Northern Indiana Poets" competition sponsored by The Progress Club of South Bend, IN.

A SONNET TO MY STAR OF HOPE

The tree is trimmed in glorious array
With tinkling bells and silver streamers fair
    And bright; and yet, the topmost branch is
                bare,
The sacred symbol of each Christmas day,
The star is gone. A thousand light beams play
From splintered crystals on the floor. I share
    In pain its loss. Hope changes to despair
    And for an over-anxious hand, I pay.

Our love, a beauteous thing; a star of hope
That topped the decorations of life's tree.
    That gave me strength and faith to face the
             cost
Of life, that buoyed my will with fate to cope;
Lies shattered. Fragments of a memory
Reminding me of all I had and lost.

OPAL

Lovely, star-kissed opal;
Iridescent gem;
Cold, appealing moonstone
Plucked from nature's hem.
Mirror of the rainbow:
Sages call you still
Bearer of bad tidings,
Harborer of ill.

Does the name you uphold
Signify your kind?
Are your eyes, so lustrous,
Useful as a blind?
Is that fair complexion,
Hiding any harm?
What is there to injure,
In your potent charm?
Many through the ages
Fell beneath its spell.
Aptly named? I wonder.
Time alone can tell.

- Published the 1939 "Patrons-of Poetry Anthology of Northern Indiana Poets" sponsored by the Progress club of South Bend, Ind.

THE GAME OF WAR
(A Farce in Three Acts)

Act 1

Scene 1: Place: Central Europe. Time: The Nineteen Thirties.

Mars, the God of War, is speaking:

Awake! Bestir! You sleeping Huns!
Your ancestry has waited long
For you to act. Make right this wrong.
And start the cry
"To do or die!"
Step forth! Make claim! And bare your guns!

Scene II: Place-same as before. Time later.

Mars speaks:

Aha! You see? How easily won
When boldness and a stalwart heart
Joined hand in hand, with sudden start
Meet caution's dare!
They cry, "Play fair",
But heed them not! You've just begun!

Act II

Scene 1:   Place: Western Europe. Time:
September 1939
Mars is speaking:
What ho! My men of English brow
Bestir yourself! Think you debate
Will quench their fire or lesson hate?
So great is cost
Of time that's lost!
Act soon! Let's have no Munich now!
Scene II: Place The Western Hemisphere.
Time – Last of 1939
Mars speaks:
To arms! To arms! To free the world
Of tyrants all! Your liberty
Is jeopardized. Democracy
Depends on you.
Join now! Be true!
And see the flag of freedom still unfurled!

Act III

Scene 1:   Place – Somewhere above Time –
Later
Mars: (laughing to himself)
The game is on! You wretched fools,
So easily duped and led astray
On pretext slight; who cast away
The right to live;
Fight on, and give
Your life's blood forth in sticky pools.

DEDICATION

If I could mold these bits of human clay

To love of all mankind through faith in God,

And hold before them in the paths they trod,

The standards of a better, brighter way;

If I could set, their faltering steps aright,

And spur their flagging strength to greater force

As they amass the lore which marks the course

That each must follow toward the distant light:

If I could lift their sights above the dross

Of life: could challenge then to seek and do

The noble deeds, which are too rarely done;

My life-'till now a question mark of loss

Or gain-would be, at death, fulfilled anew

If I but hear Him say, "Thou strived and WON!"

56

V igilantly men watched the star

I llumine the earth on a peaceful night

O ver a thousand years ago,

L aving the stable in radiance bright,

E nthralling the shepherds and guiding them

T o the Christ who was born in Bethlehem.
O ut of the heart the message still,

V aried in form, encircles the earth

E choing tidings of good will;

R e-echoing joys of the Savior's birth

M unificently this greetings brings

Y uletide wishes so warm and true

E ven the sender is richly blessed

R emembering friendly folks like you.

TO A FLOWER

Tiny, lonesome flower,
Do not hide your face,

You have struggled greatly
Living in this place.

Stones abound to cheat you;
Light has been denied.

Every shrunken leaflet
Shows the way you've tried,

Bursting buds of beauty
In a dismal cave.

You're returning tenfold
Talent that He gave.

Many human beings
If they did as well,

Could construct a heaven
Out of living hell.

IN THE DAYS OF THE VICTORY GARDEN

When you heard of plans for gardening,
Did you feel your muscles hardening
When thinking of the hoeing
And the sowing
To be done?
Did you feel a patriot's duty to
Enlist your strength and beauty to
The cause of feeding cattle
That a battle
Might be won?
Did you purchase seeds unsparingly?
Of cabbage, peas, and daringly
Some celtuce, cos, tomatoes,
And potatoes,
Corn, and beans?
Did you borrow tools repeatedly
And issue statements heatedly
As every normal friend does,
That the end was
In the means?
Did you clothe yourself most fittingly
In gloves and shorts, unwittingly
Amusing half your neighbors
With your labors
In the dirt?
Did you start your work unmincingly
And strain and sweat convincingly
Unmindful of the aching
And the breaking
And the hurt?

Just to learn that endless striving
Finds the thrifty weed still thriving
As voracious insect millions
Into billions
Multiply?
Did you then decide it's smarter
Your specific bent to barter
And not let nature kid you?
Well, did you?
So did I!

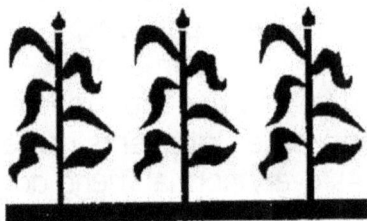

SNOWFALL

So quietly, the snow came down

Throughout the entire night.

The green of grass and earthen-brown

Were now a pristine white.

Each twig and bough had added height

As Mother Nature planned.

And we awoke to find the earth

A "Winter Wonderland."

• *Published in the 1941 "Patrons-of-Poetry Anthology of Northern Indiana Poets" competition sponsored by The Progress Club of South Bend, Ind.*

LOST

LOST   a charming miss
Whose graces I admire!
STRAYED   two pale blue eyes
That set my heart on fire!
STOLEN   from ruby lips
So warmly met above,
a kiss that lingered on,
and then returned my love!

THE TALE OF THE TANTALIZING TONGUE

"Ham-fat" I call her. "Ham-fat"!
Though she weights one hundred nine
And looks as lean and scrawny
As a tree at timberline.
"Prude" I whisper.   "Prude"!
When with youthful head held high,
Ignoring jibes and cat-calls,
She proudly marches by.
"Dim-wit"! I chide her.   "Dim-wit"'
Or "Bone-head", or "Droopy", or "Drip"!
Nothing so totally scathing
Escapes my acidulous lip.
"Worthless" I say   "Worthless"!
"And I'm glad that you're not mine.
"

But the center of my being knows
She's everything that's fine.

I HAVEN'T FORGOTTEN YET

Though days and weeks have swiftly passed
Since last the hour we met,
Your sweetness clings in my memory.
I haven't forgotten yet.
I haven't forgotten your lovely smile
Or the light that gleams in your eye,
Like candles that glow on Christmas Eve
Inspiring the passer-by.
I haven't forgotten the touch of your hand;
How a friendly, soft caress
Could soothe the restless strife within
And bring forgetfulness.
I haven't forgotten the things we did,
So intimate, tender, and true.
They're sacred still in my memory.
I haven't forgotten. Have you?

THE ANXIOUS QUEST

*
*

From
Store to
Store I made
My way,and to
Each questionnaire,-
"Yes, something in a nightie,
please. It's for a l ady,fair and-
*** Pajamas? No-o-, I'd rather not.
It's just a waste of time to look at them. ***
Oh! Crepe de chene! ** Ah, yes! They are sublime,
But then, you see, this time she said, *** "Oh no!"
No snuggies. *** I see the cut is full, but please, I want to
see
A gown, a lovely, dainty hue, with smocked appearance
at
The neck, perhaps a strap or two, in smoothest satin
Without lace. *** You're sorry? So am I"
.So if
this
garment doesn't suit
at least, you know I try.

IF I WERE YOU

If I were you. I'd cast away
My haughty air when some young lad,
Whose name is good but finance bad.
Looks longingly to have his say.
For vanity is hard to bear
In other folks, without just cause;
And snobbishness and pride are flows
When used to hurt the ones who care.
You wish to know what I would do?
I'd smile and speak if I were you.

IT'S THE LITTLE THINGS THAT COUNT

The unit of the seashore is a tiny grain of sand.
The mighty waves that fill the deep and wash the
ocean Strand.
Are fed by little drips that fall as rain upon the
land.
The myriad of brilliant stars is lovely to the sight;
And yet, attention wavers to the solitary flight
Of every shooting comet as it streaks across the
night.
A single brick is used to start construction of a
tower.
The beauty of a garden plot depends upon each
flower.
A lifetime or a thousand years is tolled off-hour by
hour.
And so, it is with each of us. It's the little things
we do
That add unto our worthiness; that test our
courage, too,
And build a lasting character, enriched, sublime,
and true.

IT'S THE LITTLE THINGS THAT COUNT

MEMORIES

I've always thought I'd write a book
About the fun we had
While boarding at the Thompson home
When "tricks" were all the fad.
You'd have to know these charming folds
To really realize
How they could tolerate our jokes
And never once chastise.
Now, Mrs. T., a friendly soul
With lots of vim and dash,
Had rented our her vacant rooms
To earn a little cash.
Four teachers from the local school
Had promptly sought her gate;
The Mrs. Thought. "Some teachers? Fine!
At least they'll be sedate."

It started out one winter's day,
At mealtime, I recall
When members of her merry house
And boarders, one and all,
Were gathered round the festive board
Which Mrs. T. prepared;
And grace was said, the bread was passed,
And conversation shared.
Then someone passed the butter plate.
My hand with thumb above
Was raised to grasp it as it came;
Then quickly with a shove

The entire golden, gooey mass
Was wrapped around my thumb,
And there I sat amid the roar,
My mouth agape but dumb.
From then on life was one mad whirl
Of plots and counter-plots.
We stitched pajamas tightly shut;
They tied ours up in knots.
We filled their bed with cracker crumbs
And thought it quite a treat.
They sprinkled ours with itching dust
That burned our legs and feet.
We emptied all their dresser drawers
And spread their stuff like dirt.
They snatched the doctor's quinine pills
And flavored our dessert.
They placed a bomb to make it stink;
They even wired the bed
So when we'd crawl between the sheets,
We'd jump right out instead.
Good doctor T., we shrewdly guessed,
Was in on much of this,
And so to play some pranks on him
Could never be amiss.
On Sunday morn he always went
To speak at Sunday school,
Perspiring freely in his zeal
To teach the Golden Rule.
Now, handkerchiefs were meant to use
And not be stitched to pants,
But somehow, somewhere, someone erred!
They knew it at a glance.

This Sunday morn he tugged and pulled;
He worked up quite a sweat,
And had his wife not come to help,
He'd still be tugging yet.
Another time a spool was boxed
And tied beneath his bed
And from the spool and out the door
There ran a long, thin thread.
The zero hour for testing came
When sleep was very near.
The thread was jerked; his lights came on,
And sounds of "Mouse" were clear.
He pulled and pushed the dresser drawers,
And sought it high and low,
But finding nothing, soon retired;
Again that rattle, slow!
"Well I declare! It's in the bed."
Once more, he searched the house,
And if you see good Doctor T.
Just ask about that "mouse"
Ah! Memories of long ago
When hearts were light and gay
And youth in constant merriment
Must fling itself away!
Each joy becomes a treasured pearl,
A perfect, priceless gem
That through the years enriches life
And forms its diadem.
To you who knew humanity
And gave such loving care,
Who looked for joys that beautify
And found them everywhere,

May you recall each little thing,
Through all the years to be,
Which made your lives on earth so much
A golden memory.

Us GOOKS

Sence Maw an'Paw hev struck it rich from
workin' in the war.
We've left that one-room shack behind an'
closed an'barred the door.
"Taint right to live like Jukes an' Joads. " Says
Paw who's might well-read;
"We're going' to live like city-swells; a life of
ease, instead.
"

So here we be! A manshum place fittin' fer a
king.
With rooms for this an' rooms fer that; why
theysa room fer everthing.
In one we set, another sleep; in one my Maw
jest cooks;
An' still another where we eats; an' one with
lots on hooks.
Paw says he'll store his guns in there- 'twill
make a darn good rack,
But Maw's fer storin'taters an'hangin'up each
sack.
The bestes' one of all the rooms is one all green
an'white
Chuck full of purty gadjets to make yerself look
bright
Why, theysa place fer washin' bodies all over all
at once;
But Maw says that's fer Sattidays, - an' only
winter months.

No need to save on water as we usta haf to
do!
I'll pull the plug an' let'er drain when us six kids
er through.
Maw plans to wash out duds up thar because
it's such a tub
That's all our grimy clothes can soak an' she
won't need to rub.
Theysa nother place fer washin' hands an' if
you wish, yer face,
But not 'till Ben removes, his fish an' finds
another place.
One thing we pondered quite a spell; some
gadjet near the wall
That no one seemed to understand er sense its
use at all
'Til Paw came up an' heered us ask. He
scratched beneath his hat,
But quickly said with much disgust, "Ya wash
yer feet in that!'
He's taken off the wooden lids. "Twas just a
waste." He said;
"An'Maw could use the upper on fer kneadin' up
the bread."
The tother one Paw tinkered with an' made a
picsher frame;
It's hangin'in the lower hall with Granpaws face
an' name.
Oh, money is a blessing! T'would even help the
Jukes
To raise their living' standard the way it has us
Gooks!

LIMERICKS AND SCHOOL DAZE

There once was an arrongant tyke
Who in studies had gone on a strike,
But the air was soon fanned
On the place that was planned
For the "sit-down" of laggardly Mike.

There was a young lady whose yen
Was not on her studies but men
Her textbook on health
Lay untouched on the shelf.
Now she's taking it over again!

Hermin, the vermin, is squirmin'.
The apple he chewed had a worm in.
He started to laugh
'Til he found there was half
Of the squirmin' worm in Hermin!

The principal strode to the door
Bent on stilling the DIN and the ROAR;
"Where's your teacher", he lazed!
"Who's your teacher?" was dazed
When "You are, sir!" meekly came from the
floor.

His success on a horn was disputeless,
Until some wished his efforts were fruitless
It happened that might
And the saying were right
" A toothless tooter is tootless!

A little word with letters three;
A bait for squirrels beneath a tree;
It starts with "N" and ends with "T"
What can this little tree-fruit be
Which so describes my thoughts of thee?

(Untitled Poem?)

I kissed my heart goodbye
As it pattered down the floor
With trembling hand held high
To knock upon your door.
My tear-drained eyes beheld
Its shambling, weary feet
Half-turned away as though
To beat a mock retreat.
One look you gave. Tis then I knew.
My heart had said goodbye
For it belongs to you.
You smiled. And so do I.